DEDICATION

This book is dedicated to my three beautiful children who I hope will be very happy whatever careers and lifestyle they choose.

Live Well, Spend Less.

Alana Wilson

CONTENTS

Live Well, Spend Less.

ACKNOWLEDGMENTS

This book has been a few years in the making, I did not really appreciate at the beginning what writing a book entailed. Over time it has changed direction slightly, it has evolved into the book I wanted it to be.
With working full time, having three young children, a husband and a dog it has not always been easy to create the time needed, but I have got there eventually.
I have always wanted to try and help those that may feel their finances are out of their control. Those that do not really think about the way they spend their money and how they could spend it wiser. Those that do the same thing with their spending, but expect a different outcome.
I feel very strongly that it is important for people to know how to live within their means and to keep their finances in check. It can reduce stress and give you peace of mind.
I wanted to let people know they do have options they may just need to change their mindset.

I am deeply thankful to all my family.
My husband and our three amazing children for always being there for me and for believing in me.
My mum & dad for making sure I understood the value of money and for always supporting me in everything I do.
My two sisters and my brother for their ongoing support and for indirectly providing me with material for my book over the years, especially the IOU's in my money box!
I will always be grateful to my husband and my best friend for not making me feel crazy when I first said I wanted to write a book and to my parents & children when I told them I had written one!
Special thanks to my mum for proof reading this book for me.

I love you all very much indeed.

1 INTRODUCTION

Whatever your circumstances and whatever your age, it is important to be smart with your money and to know and to be content with where each penny of your money is being spent.

Whether you are self-employed, a full time employee, a part time employee, in full time education, a stay at home parent, retired or unemployed, basically whatever you currently do, if you have an income you need to make sure you are spending it in the right way to meet your (& your family's) needs.

As an Accountant with over 20 years' experience I know how important it is to make sure you keep a check on the money you have coming in and on the money you have going out. Even if this is, for no other reason, than making sure nobody else is spending your money for you!

It is never too early or too late to start keeping a track of your money and your spending. To make sure that you are confident you are spending your money wisely and that you are in control of your finances.

People that have a lot of disposable income might think they do not need to bother keeping track of their finances, but it is still important that they are aware of their spending and that they are happy with their choices.

It's sometimes people in this privileged position, that do not realise how much money they are spending on certain things. It may not be until it is brought to their attention that they actually realise they may be wasting a proportion of their money and often a larger proportion than they would have imagined.

People with a lower income may already be all too aware of where their money goes. As they may already have to make decisions on a daily basis of what they can live without and what they really do need. They may already be very savvy with their money and their spending, but are always open to new advice and tips on how they can help themselves further.

The one thing that is certain is that it is equally important to know where your money is going, whatever your circumstances and life style.

Whether you have a lot of money or a little.

So that you can make sure that your money works hard for you, in the same way that you work hard for it. We all work hard or have worked hard for our income, whatever we do or have done. Therefore it is in our own interest to look after our income and spend it in the best way we can.

Everyone should be in control of their finances and if you do not currently feel you are, it is time to take control.

Before you start, it is important to have a clear perspective on the things that give value to your life. We all know it is not the material things that we have that are most important to us, that give us true happiness and contentment.

Always remember, if you have your health, family, friends, somewhere warm and dry to stay, food and are safe, that is a very good position to be in and we need to remind ourselves of this!

There are people in the world that do not have their health and this in itself would no doubt be a time in their lives when reality hits home. When they contemplate the important things in their lives and I imagine none of those things that come to the fore are the material possession they have accumulated.

Some people do not have family. They may feel very alone and again know how lucky those that do have family are, to have the unconditional love and support in their lives.

We are all too aware that there are people who do not have a safe, dry and warm place to stay. Through no fault of their own and who will know just how lucky people are that know when they will next eat and that they have a place to call home.

So we all need to remember how very fortunate we are if we do have these things already in our lives. Money is important, but it is by no means the whole picture.

We can all get swept up at times in wanting more than we have and more than we actually need and can forget about what we already have.

It may be nice to have certain things, but if your budget means you cannot or that you will have to forgo other things in order to have these things, take some time to think about what it is you REALLY NEED?

This is not to say that we should not have dreams. It's good to have dreams, we are human after all. So if you have dreams and you want to be able to work towards your goal, use that dream as the motivation for getting your finances in a position to allow you to achieve it or at least get as close as you are able to that dream.

2 IF YOU HAVE A DREAM

If you have a dream you may need to fully understand your finances to know if it will be possible to achieve. Especially if it is a big dream.

You may dream about being debt free. Buying a first home. Getting married. Having children. Going on holiday!

You may be dreaming of being mortgage free.

Dreaming of moving away, buying a new car, moving to a bigger home.

It may be a smaller dream you have, of buying your child the present they want for their birthday. Or buying a nice new outfit for that special occasion.

You may have a very big dream that seems impossible.

You may be a working parent and dream of reducing your hours to spend more time with your family. Whilst knowing you need to work to earn the money that you do to keep the standard of living you currently have. It may not be an overly luxurious lifestyle, so to reduce your income would hit your family significantly.

You may dream of changing jobs, knowing the money is less, but you would enjoy the work more.

The list of what we may be dreaming about is endless and many of the dreams will rely on money and us managing our finances well to achieve them.

The majority of us work to have the level of lifestyle that our salary allows us to have. This may be food on the table, clean clothes and a roof over our head. It may include running a car, meals out now and again and an annual holiday. Or it may be a life of pure luxury.

We often hear the saying that you should work to live not live to work, but we all know that due to the demands both financially and on our time, this can be very difficult to fully embrace at times.

If your dream seem impossible right now you may need to break it down into smaller steps in order to see a route to achieving it.

If you have a dream, big or small, but at this current moment you cannot see a way of achieving it, do not panic or give up!

It is important to fully understand where you currently are financially to know what your options are.

Bigger dreams may take longer to achieve than smaller dreams. If this is the case you will need to understand and accept this.

Always remember to remind yourself of what you do have and be thankful, life feels better when we focus on the positive.

3 NEW BEGINNINGS

You may not actually be dreaming of anything at this moment, but you are at the beginning of a new chapter in your life and therefore in a position where you would like to understand how to manage your finances for yourself. It may be your first steps into independence!

You may be going off to University and need to survive on a low income, so you want to know how to keep your finances under control and use your money in the best way you possibly can.

You may be at the beginning of your working life, just starting out and you are keen to make sure you know how to look after the money you will be earning. So as to provide the best life for yourself that you can afford.

You may be approaching a time in your life where you are considering retiring and want some hints and ideas for making your money go as far as possible.

You may have been working for a while and your income seems to have to spread that little bit further now than it did before. Your finances might be getting tighter, so you need some idea's to help alleviate some of the pressure on them.

You, a relationship, or partner, may have got you into debt, now or in the past and you want to get yourself out of debt or avoid getting back into debt.

A change may have been forced on you, an unexpected change, redundancy or job loss, divorce, ill-health, meaning you now need to change your spending habits.

You may now be on universal credits which is paid monthly and has replaced the previously weekly paid benefit. This may be the reason you need to learn to budget your money to last the month rather than just a week.

Whether you are starting a new chapter in your life, leaving home, getting your first job, going to university, going travelling, retiring, having a baby. Basically any situation where you have to be responsible for your own money for the first time. Or where you are needing to live on a lower budget than previously. This can be both an exciting and a daunting time.

You may not be looking to tighten your belt due to a dream you have, or a change in your life, you may have worked hard for many years, always been pretty good with your money and you would just like to see if there are any other ways you have not thought about that could help you make some savings.

Whatever your reason for wanting to be smarter with your money and for buying this book, well done, you have taken the first step to becoming more savvy with your money.

4 WHO SHOULD KEEP A CHECK OF THEIR FINANCES?

Who should keep a check of their finances? Everyone! Everyone should keep a check on their finances.

Some people tend to be considered good with money and some people are considered to be bad with money. What makes a person good or bad with money?

Are you good or bad with money due to your level of earnings/income?

Or maybe due to your personality?

Do some people worry about being or getting into debt so they do all they can to avoid it?

Is it due to being taught at a younger age to value money?

Is it due to a person's age and stage of life?

Or due to the fact some people may not care, debt does not worry them?

It could possibly be down to them thinking if others can have those things then so can they, even if it means taking on debt to get them.

The urge to have something may be greater than the knowledge you cannot afford it?

I do not know the answer. I imagine it is part nature and part nurture. As my older sister and I were brought up in the same household with the same values. When we were younger and even in days where we were given pocket money, I would save for anything I bought, whereas my sister would find a way to get what she wanted straight away. I quite often found IOU's in my money box from her!

Whatever the reason people are considered to be good or bad with money, the good thing is all of us can be good with money if we want to be and if we are prepared to take the right steps!!

It is definitely a misconception to think that those with lower incomes are more likely to get themselves into financial difficulty. As mentioned previously, those with less can be very pennywise and know exactly where all their money goes and what they need their money for. They can be very creative at making their money go further, because they have had to be.

It is also a misconception to think that those with more money are better with money. As those with money can be very irresponsible with it! This may be due to them believing there will always be more. It may be because they have got used to a certain lifestyle or are seen to have a certain lifestyle and they need, want or choose, to keep up the appearance.

Think of certain celebrities that we hear about on the news that have got themselves into financial difficulties. If you are like me, you may wonder how, with all they will have earned and possibly still do earn, have they managed to get themselves in to such a mess financially.

It is proof that whatever your circumstances, if you do not live within your means and you are not aware of your spending, whatever your income you can get yourself in a difficult financial situation.

Whatever your income level, if you do not keep a check of your spending, it is easy for money to be spent without thinking.

It's the same checks for everyone too. It just may be for different reasons.

Those with less money may need to keep a check to make sure they can afford everything they need, all their essential costs.

Those with more money may need to keep a check to make sure they are not wasting their disposable income and to continue to make sure they can afford the lifestyle they live.

Those with *a lot* of money, again need to keep a check to avoid wasting money, but also so they can invest and make sure they have their money in the liquid form they require it. Whilst earning at the best rate they can on their funds.

What if you are already in financial difficulty?

If you are constantly thinking it would be okay if you had more money. Going round in circles trying to work out how to get more money, but are still drawing a blank. Consider speaking to a close friend or family member. Even if they cannot help financially they may make you look at things differently or suggest something you have not thought of. Together you can consider what your options are to start working towards getting your finances stable.

A problem shared is a problem halved.

If you are thinking I could not speak to anyone about my financial situation, do not be embarrassed about it, the people that love and care for you will be more than happy to listen. To offer you advice, *if wanted*, and to try to support you through your difficult time. Remember, accepting you have a problem is the start of you finding a solution.

Remember it is never too late to start getting your finances in order.

If you do not have anyone to talk to, but would like help seek whatever help is available, via your local citizen's advice bureau, council or charities. There are often places to go where you can get advice and support.

Do not think, I got myself into this, I have to get myself out of it. Help is available because sometimes in our lives we need it. Rest assured you will not be the only one in your situation.

It will be a revelation for you when you accept that this might be a time you need help and you get access to the help you need. It will be like a weight is lifted. Feeling supported in your journey to sort your finances out will help you no end.

As you start to pay off your debts you will feel more and more empowered which will spur you on to continue.

Whatever your reason for wanting to be in control of your finances, it is a step in the right direction making the decision to start taking control. So be proud of yourself for making the decision to start!

5 WHAT DOES TAKING CONTROL OF YOUR FINANCES MEAN?

After deciding you are going to take control, the next step to taking control of your finances, is simply knowing what money you have coming in and what money you have going out.

A great place to start is with a simple budget.

Prepare a budget.........

How do you do this?

What is a budget?

A budget is about knowing what money you have coming in and what you can and cannot afford. Sounds simple? That is because it is. You literally need to write down your income and outgoings and expectations for future weeks or months, depending on if your income is weekly or monthly.

This may sound a bit boring. If boring means being in total control of you money, I guess you may consider it boring. However, the truth of it is that having clarity of where you stand financially, gives you options! Options of what you can afford to do, and what you cannot. So you are aware of what your decisions mean for you financially when you make them.

It can give you a sense of freedom, being in control, so it is anything but boring in reality.

It will seriously give you a new found strength and determination.

A budget can be as simple or as detailed as you like and can be updated or referred to as much or as little as you believe is necessary.

There is no need for it to take over your life, but it can be there to help you make good decisions and to help you plan ahead.

Some people work two or three jobs to keep the roof over their heads and food on the table and they naturally budget, without realising, as they count every penny and make that money work hard for them. They will always know what they have for food shopping and will not go a penny over, they will keep an eye on the electric meter, turning off electrical items that are not being used to keep their costs down. Planning meals and keeping a check on portion size and snacking.

They will be in control and make their money spread as far as they can.

People who may have more disposable income, may not think twice about paying £3.50 for a coffee when they have coffee at home in the cupboard. Or £6 for a glass of wine when they can buy a bottle for the same amount. Therefore they can be more likely to spend (waste!) money without thinking about it.

If you have ever watched a TV series where they look at peoples shopping habits and the brands they purchase in their weekly shopping. Nearly all of the people that go on the programme are shocked when they find out how much they spend weekly. It goes to show that sometimes people that have a bit more disposable income may not be aware of where their money goes and may not be as careful with their money.

Many of the people on the show would pop to the shop regularly, rather than doing one big shop, therefore not realising how much in total they spend as they spend a little at a time. Some people did not plan the family meals buying on impulse and potentially spending more. There were others on the show that believed they could not change their shopping habits as their children would not eat other foods. Or they themselves did not believe cheaper products would be as nice or as good as the more expensive ones.

It seems all too easy for us, at times, to spend money without really thinking it through properly.

Taking control, means knowing where you are spending your money and being comfortable with you choices.

It is easy to see why some of us may not be in control.

In years gone by, if you bought an item you used it until it broke or it wore out. You tended to buy things you needed rather than just because you wanted them.

We now live in a much more throwaway society. An item might not be fashionable any longer even if you have only worn it twice. You may want to change a room's décor to something you have seen in a magazine even though the décor you have is perfectly fine.

We are bombarded daily, whether on social media, television adverts, in magazines, in newspapers and in many other mediums, of lovely products we should purchase. Alongside those advertisements are adverts for payday loans and credit cards and pay nothing for a year store credit cards.

This sends a message that it is okay to have things you cannot afford right now, as you can deal with the money aspect later. This can encourage people to stretch themselves financially. If you had to turn up with the money in your pocket to pay for the item you would sensibly know whether or not you could afford it. As, instead, you may just have to sign a piece of paper you can have it now and worry about whether or not you can afford it later. Later is, however, too late to discover you cannot actually afford it as you are legally bound to pay by that time.

A prior colleague of mine moved into their first rented flat with their partner and on the first weekend they went and signed themselves up to new credit agreements, for a TV, sofa and other furniture and white goods. They then got themselves so stressed as they struggled to pay the monthly finance and ended up going off work due to the stress. This could have been avoided if they had looked at their earnings, the costs they have to cover with the additional finance and seeing if they were able to comfortably afford the finance before they had signed themselves up for it. Instead they looked at the shiny new products and were seduced.

Many of us do strive to have a nice home, a nice car, holidays, fashionable clothes and all the other things we see online, on television and in magazines and newspapers.

However, the reality is that it is not about thinking if you had more money life would be better, like I have already mentioned, it is about making sure you make your money work the best it can for you and you being in control of it rather than the other way round.

Yes I am sure for many of us more money would be nice, but the reality is that unless you have a way of getting this extra money, let's not dwell on it, let's concentrate on what you do have!

If you are about to move out and have been looking at new items, consider looking at free and cheaper options. Borrow furniture from family and friends, look on second hand site. Replace with new as your finances allow, if you still want to. Remember you will be so happy to be in your own place you do not need to do it all and have everything right now.

If however, it is too late and you have taken on more credit than you feel comfortable with, please speak to someone you trust and get some help to work out what you can afford and how you will get yourself through this.

If you are younger you may be able to consider moving back home with your parents in order to reduce your costs. Consider selling the items you purchased for the best price you can get to aid paying the debt off.

Increase your income if you are able to. Consider changing jobs (if this is a real option and natural progression in your career), or work overtime if you are able to.

Whatever your financial position, if, to meet your goal, be it a dream, a change in situation, or paying off debt, you need more money and there is nothing you can do to change the amount of money you have coming in, adjusting what you spend is going to be key.

If you can increase your disposable income by increasing your income or by adjusting your spending you are on your way to making your dream, new chapter or change, a reality.

Consider everything that you have available to you and that could be available to you and then work out how to use it as effectively as you can. Start to take the control.

6 WHY TAKE CONTROL OF YOUR FINANCES?

Why gain control of your finances?

Well I have probably answered this already several times, but in simple terms it is all about knowing what you have to spend and deciding what you need to spend it on. It helps you to prioritise your spending and think more about future expenses. It will also hopefully help you avoid wasting your money. It therefore allows you the peace of mind that you can meet your living costs weekly/monthly and helps you plan for those ad hoc expenses.

Another good reason is because not doing so could lead to financial difficulty and being in financial difficulty can be very stressful and potentially affect your health and your relationships.

In my role as an accountant in industry, I have seen many an employee ask for loans to get them through the month. Some due to broken down cars and unexpected vet bills that they could not have known would happen. Others for Christmas presents and prom dresses, which they quite clearly could have planned for.

The unexpected costs I do have great sympathy for as I know what it is like to have a boiler, washing machine or car break down or an out of the blue vet bill and if you have not got a rainy day fund or savings, it's hard to juggle your finances to meet the additional cost.

The prom dress, though, is another matter!

This is a true story! We were asked to loan money so an employee could buy their daughter a prom dress. As a caring employer we did not want to see our employee or the employee's daughter let down and not get the dress she wanted. So we did on this occasion lend the money. We were however a little disappointed in our employee that they had not realised, months before, when they first knew about the prom, that they would need to start to save for the dress they wanted to buy their daughter.

It was also disappointing to see that they felt it was the right decision to borrow the money and buy the more expensive dress rather than lowering their daughters expectation with the price of the dress she could purchase. Maybe considering a second hand dress, as let's be honest most of these dresses are only worn once, so second hand in this case is as good as new. Instead they made a decision to get into debt for the dress.

Also frustrating in this story is that each day this particular employee would be outside at the snack van purchasing food for their day. Think about it, even if they only spent £2 a day, over a four working month period they could have saved £160 plus, just by not spending money on snacks. Even if they had to bring their own food in from home, which I realise they would have to purchase still this would have easily saved them £100 at the end of the four months.

Please do not even get me started about the request for help for Christmas presents…….. being asked for a loan so an employee could buy their child a games console for Christmas! Christmas is the same day every year, this should not be a surprise to anyone!

I totally understand that Christmas is an expensive time of the year. So planning ahead is very important as it is *always* an expensive time of year.

If you are on a tight budget, manage your expectations, be realistic and manage your family and friend's expectations when it comes to presents. *See later in the book.*

As an accountant giving a loan to any employee always makes me want to offer budgeting advice to help them in the future. Which I have done at times! Having a loan may seem like the right thing to do at the time, but I think ahead and know we are just making it harder on the person the next month when they get paid and now need to repay the loan. As then the employee is short in their pay that month and possibly longer depending on the terms the loan is to be repaid under.

Once you get into debt it is so much harder to pay it off. Think about it, if you were saving for a new car, putting that £100 a month away knowing it is moving you that bit closer to your goal is exciting. Your new car gives you a goal to motivate you to work for.

If however, you purchase that car on finance, once you have driven a brand new car off the fore court, but are still paying for it three years later at £100 per month and there may be a newer car you like, or other things you want to spend that £100 per month on. Paying the £100 each month is not exciting at all!

You may be in a position where you still have loads to pay off on the car, but you no longer feel that thrill of excitement you had when you went and signed the paper to be able to drive your car away.

Its all about accepting upfront the enormity of what you will be taking on.

Therefore this is not to say you should not take finance. If and only if, you are able to afford the finance and you have looked at your other options and you still decide buying something on finance is the right decision for the right reasons. Then, of course, it is your prerogative.

However, I would always suggest in addition to considering if you can keep up the payments for the term of the agreement and looking at other options, you also try and consider your position in a few years, when you are still going to be repaying the debt. Will the car still be as important as it is now, how will your life have changed and will this effect what you want to spend your money on? If after thinking about all these things you still want to sign the paper and take the finance that is of course your decision.

When I was younger I brought a brand new car on finance and I loved it! When I was still paying off the finance a couple of years later, but by then I was engaged to be married and I was wanting to save for our wedding rather than pay for a car. Although I have to be honest I did still love my car. Anyway, I had to sell the car, pay off the finance with the sale proceeds and then I could save for the wedding, which had become the top priority. Luckily I covered the finance completely with the sale proceeds I received, but not by a lot and this may quite easily have not been the case. So do bear in mind, that things do change, especially when looking at signing up to any longer term credit.

Only enter any finance commitments with your eyes fully open, however much or little you earn

One thing is evident, even though money cannot buy you the important things in life, it is without doubt a major part of all of our lives. Therefore making sure you take control and keep in control of your finances is very important.

7 WHEN SHOULD YOU START TO TAKE CONTROL OF YOUR FINANCES?

When should you start taking control of your finances?

Now!

Maybe next week or next month when you have a bit more time?

No, now!

Straight after you are next paid, as you have not got much left in your bank account right now?

No, now!

After Christmas as this is a very busy and expensive month? etc……

No! Do not put it off, there is no time like the present!

Take control right now!

Get a pen, a piece of paper, a calculator and a calendar, alternatively if you have access to a computer open a new spreadsheet ready to start straight away.

Never put off till tomorrow what you can do today!

8 HOW DO YOU START TO TAKE CONTROL OF YOUR FINANCES?

Once you have the pen and paper or the spreadsheet open ready, how do you start?.......

Start by listing all the types of income you receive each week or month, depending on the frequency of your income. This will include any income you have, salary, child allowance, dividends, interest, maintenance, etc. Next to the type of income put the value of that income and once you have listed all the types and put a value next to them total it up.

Basically if you are paid monthly and your payments are mostly monthly work your budget monthly, if you are paid weekly and your costs are weekly work it weekly, four-weekly budget four-weekly and so on.

Underneath the income, list the expenses you have monthly, such as rent, mortgage, council tax, utilities (water, gas, electric), food shopping, petrol, insurance, telephone/mobile, TV licence, childminder, kids clubs, pension, TV packages, etc. At this point only include the must have's and again total.

If you have a mix of weekly and monthly costs or incomes, do not fret. If you spend £100 on food weekly, work out what day you shop on and the number of those days in the particular month you are calculating. Multiple the weekly amount by the amount of those days in the month to get your monthly amount.

For example if you shop on a Friday and there are four Fridays in February this year, your monthly cost in February would be £400 for food shopping (£100*4).

You can use this calculation if your income is weekly, but most of your expenses are monthly so you want a monthly budget. Again work out the day you get paid each week and how many of those days are in the month you are working out. Then multiply the number of days in that month by the amount of weekly income, to get your monthly total.

For example if you earn £300 per week and get paid on a Saturday, if there are 5 Saturdays in that particular month your income would be £1,500 (£300*5).

Once you have all your incomes totaled and your expenses totaled you then do a simple sum of income less expenses.

Income total - Essential expenses total = Balance

Hopefully you will find that the income is higher than the outgoings at this stage and assuming this is the case, the difference between the income and the expenses gives you the money you have available to you until your next pay day. This balance is to spend on things other than the essential expenses you have listed or put by for future costs, or in savings or in your pension.

If you have other monthly costs that you did not consider essential, but you do intend to keep spending on, then total these up and again subtract this amount from the balance you got to after the previous calculation.

Balance - Non Essential expenses = New Balance.
If you do have an amount left a week or a month, you then may want to put a certain amount away either weekly or monthly towards costs that you do not have right now, but that you know you will have to meet in the future.
Such as birthdays, Christmas, a holiday, school uniform and school shoe shop, etc. Then when it comes to paying for these you can relax in the knowledge you have saved for it as you have gone along and have it covered.

Obviously the amount you decide to put aside for these will depend on what expectations you have of these costings. For example if you expect to spend £X at Christmas, £X on birthdays during the year, £X on a holiday and £X on school uniform and it totals say £3,000 for the year, you know monthly you would need to save £250 (£3000/12), or weekly you would need to save £57 (£3000/52).

Assuming after essential costs, non essential costs and annual costs you still have a positive balance it would be sensible to build yourself a rainy day fund, for any unexpected expenses. Such as a broken appliance, car repairs, vet bills, etc. To do this, put an amount each month aside, into a separate savings account if possible. It can be as little or as much as you can afford, it's just in case something unexpected comes up.

Example of a budget:

Monthly Income	Salary	£2270
	Child Benefit	£200
	Other	£50
	TOTAL	**£2520**

Monthly Expenses	Rent/Mortgage	£900
(Essential)	Rates	£200
	Utility bills	£200
	Food	£500
	Car/Petrol	£250
	Insurance	£50
	TV Licence	£15
(Non Essential)	TV package	£40
	Savings (Rainy day)	£50
	Birthdays/Xmas savings	£50
	Vet/Pet	£15
Weekly spending money (£20/£25pw)		£100
	Holiday fund	£50
	TOTAL	**£2420**

Income less Expenses = Balance per month £100 excess a month (the buffer).

Make sure whatever you decide to allow for the above mentioned funds you leave yourself enough to have a weekly or monthly buffer, in your bank or pocket. Just in case your weekly spend is already allocated and does not cover those little extras. Such as a forgotten packed lunch, parking, a treat, a donation, a drink with friends, an extra trip to the supermarket as you have run out of something earlier than expected, a child's school trip you have just found out about, etc.

There are always things that pop up that you were not aware of and this money is to cover those things. If you don't spend it you can roll it over to the next month. Especially if you know you have a busy month coming up, you may choose to roll it over.

The balance (the buffer) should be broken down into a weekly or a monthly spend, whatever suits you best. So if you have say £100 per month for incidentals like in the above example, it works out at £23 a week over the year (100*12/52). If you spend none of the £100 in the first week of the month you know you have more than the £23pw for the later weeks in the month. Or if you spend more in the first week you know you have to be more careful for the rest of the month as you will have less than the £23pw.

Being aware that you only have that set amount, will make you think differently and it will make you question decisions you may have previously just made without thinking about.

For example if you are in a supermarket to grab some milk and you see a magazine, chocolate, bottle of wine, top, face cream, kids toy, etc that you think oh I'll just grab that whilst I am here. If you know you only have £100 for the whole month and you have already spent £75 of it, you will question whether you really need what you are considering buying! And only buy it if you have concluded that you do and that you are willing to forego something else, which might come up later in the month, for it.

One of the first rules to being in control of your finances, is being aware of what you have to spend and what you need to spend it on, not just spending until your bank account is empty, as this will often lead to you needing to borrow.

Family and friends may be happy to lend on the odd occasion, but if it becomes regular, too much is required, or you struggle to repay them when you say you will, they may not be so happy to lend to you again. This may mean you end up needing to resort to other short term financing which is often very expensive.

Also if you owe people money and then they see you spending money without a second thought to the money you owe them, they may become very resentful.

You can, if you are up for it, set up a budget where you start with your bank balance as it currently is. This gives you an ongoing running total that you can check to your bank account regularly. So start with your bank balance after everything has cleared that you have currently paid. Then add your payments and your income, so you can keep a running total of your bank balance monthly. This can be spanned over many months so you can plan ahead for those more costly months very accurately.

Example budget starting with your current bank balance:

		Jan	Feb
Bank Balance brought forward		**£240**	**£340**
Monthly Income	Salary	£2270	£2270
	Child Benefit	£200	£200
	Other	£50	£50
	TOTAL	**£2520**	**£2520**
Monthly Expenses	Rent/Mortgage	£900	£900
(Essential)	Rates	£200	£200
	Utility bills	£200	£200
	Food	£500	£500
	Car/Petrol	£250	£250
	Insurance	£50	£50
	TV Licence	£15	£15
(Non Essential)	TV package	£40	£40
	Savings (Rainy day)	£50	£50
	Christmas/Birthdays savings	£50	£50
	Vet/Pet	£15	£15
Weekly spending money (£20/£25pw)		£100	£100
	Holiday fund	£50	£50
	TOTAL	**£2420**	**£2420**
Bank Balance carried forward		**£340**	**£440**

At the end of each month you can agree your balance to your actual bank account.

And if you want to check your progress part way through

the month, just take the bank balance you began with, add the income you have received so far and subtract the expenses you have paid so far, this should agree to your actual bank balance.

If you only have one bank account so any savings or money you put by for future expenses needs to remain in the bank account you have, you will see your balance grow.

You will then need to keep a little breakdown of what that balance is made up of, which you can do underneath your income less expenses calculation. It will help you to keep track of how much you have put by for each potential future cost and to remember it is already allocated and not just there for you to spend.

Basically if you end January with £340, like in the above example, if you have a costs & savings of £165 that you have accounted for in the monthly budget, but you have not *actually* spent you should have £340+£165=£505 in your bank at the end of the month. At the end of February you should have £440 (the end of February balance) plus £165 from January and £165 from February, for costs not actually spent, so £770 in total.

Example breaking down savings and unspent expenses:

	Jan	Feb
Bank Balance carried forward	**£340**	**£440**
Extra in Bank		
Christmas/Birthday savings	£50	£100
Savings (Rainy day)	£50	£100
Vet/Pet costs	£15	£30
Holiday fund	£50	£100
Actual Bank Balance	**£505**	**£770**

Bank balance = the expected bank balance per the previous example.
Extra in bank = all the costs that were budgeted for but not *actually* spent in the month in question.

9 WHERE ARE YOUR FINANCES AT?

The calculations we have done so far have assumed the Income less Expenses balance is positive! If that is the case that is great, but what if that is not the case?

If you get a negative balance when you do the sums, do not worry. This is where you need to consider what on your non-essential list of expenses you can reduce, do less frequently or stop completely.

Hopefully there will be some non essential items you are prepared to give up or reduce to bring your balance positive.

Work out what non essential costs you would drop if you were able to keep other ones. For example the gym membership may go if you have one, as you can replace it with a cheaper option, such as a run. However, you may not be prepared to give up your monthly night out with friends.

If there are no costs you are prepared to give up or reduce on your non essential costs, you need to consider what your other options are. Can you reduce your essential costs, by making different choices? Can you increase your income?

There are options and you will get a clearer picture of what options are available to you by knowing where your finances are currently at.

See 'What if the balance is negative?' later in the book.

However, you may be in the financial position where you can meet all your essential and non essential costs, including having a rainy day fund and with a little left over.

Or your financial position may easily cover all your costs and leave you with lots of money left over.

Wherever your finances fall, it is important to make sure you keep a check on going, as costs can creep up over time, so make sure you continue to know what your financial position is.

Alternatively you may find you get a large increase in income, moving you into a different financial situation.

If you have an income that allows you to have all the buffers you need for weekly/monthly costs, money put by for annual costs and savings for unexpected costs this is a very positive place to be at. It still makes sense to make sure you are getting the most out of your money and spending it wisely. So you still need to make sure you are keeping a check on your money.

If your income gives you a huge disposable income, a sensible thing to do now would be to write down what you spend your disposable income on, in a year. Then see if you feel you get that much benefit out of it!

For example if you find you have £1,000 a month, so £12,000 a year excess, think what that could mean for you, that could buy a car, a fantastic holiday, or even both. If that amount is spent over the year and at the end of the year you do not really know what on, this is the time for you to find out and to start controlling your finances and to stop letting yourself spend your money without proper consideration of what it is going on.

This amount of money should not just slip through your fingers without you knowing what on, not even £500 should slip through your fingers a year without you knowing what on!

If you are in the privileged position of having a very large £1,000 per month excess. Think how much it would amount to over five years if you saved it! Think how it could reduce your mortgage, if you have one, if you chose to overpay rather than allow yourself to spend the money because it is there.

Saying that, if you are in the situation, that when looking at it, you believe you have been wasting your money on frivolous things, then do not dwell on it. You cannot change what you have been doing with the money. So just be resolute that from now on you are wise to it and that going forward you will *not* do the same.

It's not unusual for those with higher disposable incomes to have more expensive cars that cost more to run. More clothes and shoes that are more expensive. To go out for meals and nights out more frequently, have more frequent breaks and holidays. Have take-aways more often, drink champagne and other more expensive drinks and have pamper and beauty treatments. All without thinking or realising the total of their income that is spent on these things over a year.

Budgeting brings out where your finances are at currently and allows you to consider where you would like them to be.

If you work out you spend a fortune on going out each year, but you can afford it and you consider it money well spent, obviously that is your choice.

If you are spending lots of money unnecessarily and you have something different you would like to spend your money on from now on, you can make different choices going forward.

This is the whole point of understanding where your money is going, so every time you spend your money you are doing it with your eyes well and truly open. If you are happy with where you spend your money and you can afford to continue that is fine.

10 TAKING CONTROL

Now you know the basics.

Really get to know the income you have, the outgoings you have and any balance left over, big or small.

Think about it when you are spending your money.

Every time you make a purchase be it online or in a shop. Every time you get your purse or wallet out to buy something, think whether you really need to make this purchase. If not, then think whether you really want to make the purchase even though you have decided you do not need it! Was it in your budget, if not, where is that money coming from and what else may you have to give up to have it?

Take a bit of time to think about it. If you are in a supermarket, leave the item on the shelf or rack and finish getting the bits you specifically went to the shop for and the bits you did need, then decide whether you are going to go back and make the extra purchase or leave it.

If you are purchasing online, leave it in your basket whilst you do other things and then go back later if you have concluded you still want the item. I have left a full online basket many a time, having distracted myself with doing something else and by the time I have time to go back and complete it, I have changed my mind. That shows me I didn't really need the item, or maybe I did just not right then so was able to delay the purchase. Many of the times I leave a full basket is because I have something else to do, rather than me thinking I will take time to think, but it goes to show you, that impulse buys, sometimes lose their attraction when you take some time out.

It's a good idea not to save your debit or credit card details when you shop online. Or remove your credit/debit card details from online accounts, if you have already set them up. It means it takes that little bit extra effort to buy something and that effort might put you off the purchase.

Retail therapy is a real thing, so do not shop when you are stressed as you could end up spending more than you planned purely to make yourself feel better.

It's important to remember, just because you may have calculated that you have a balance of £X to spend each month, it does not mean that you actually have to spend it all.

You may decide to try and challenge yourself to see if you can spend as little as possible of your balance in a month. With the extra you have saved you could decide what you would like to do with it, be it extra in your savings, pay an extra amount off your mortgage or keep it to use in a future month when you know you have a lot planned and may need more than the balance you will have available for that month.

It can be kind of fun to challenge yourself and see how much you can have left at the end of the week or month. When you set this task for yourself, see how differently you think about it when you enter a shop and something catches your eye.

Think what you would rather do with that money and how

it would serve you best.

Compare one month to another, if you have not taken much notice of your spending one month, work out how much of your buffer you spent in total. Then set yourself a month where you will be determined to spend as little as possible, see the difference in the spend. If the difference is large try and remember why your spending was so large in the previous month and decide whether it was worth it, or needed, or not. This can spur you on to keep a check on your spending.

Even little things that you spend money on build up over time, you may think it's just a couple of pounds here and there, but this can still build up.

One thing I have noticed from my time being an accountant is that people, who sometimes cannot afford it, will spend money on things that they could easily find a cheaper, just as good, alternative option for.

For example the mobile snack van at work I mentioned earlier. It is easy for employees to go out to the snack van that comes round daily and buy a snack, when you think it's only a couple of pounds on each occasion!

If you take the employee I spoke about earlier, they probably spent at least a couple of pounds each working day at the snack van. That over a year was probably around £500.

When it came to Christmas and a certain employee, who frequented the snack van daily, asked to borrow money from the Company to buy a gaming station for their child, (yes it was the same employee that asked for the prom dress)! As again they did not want to disappoint their child, but they did not have the money to buy it. If they had been thinking and had been aware of their money and had produced a simple budget to keep a check their monthly incomings and outgoings. Taking into consideration known annual costs, such as Christmas, they could have planned to not waste £10, at least, a week on snacks. When they could quite easily bring a packed lunch and extra snacks from home and save money, probably at the very least, half the money spent at the snack van. In turn they would then not have needed to borrow the money. Borrowing which in turn left them short for the next few months whilst they paid it back, meaning they had to ask to borrow again.

Such an easy thing to give up too, well in my opinion! They would buy a warm sausage roll. When a pack of 6 or more sausage rolls from a supermarket probably costs less than one from the van. The employee had access to a free microwave so could warm their supermarket sausage roll up if they wanted to. They also had free tea and coffee available to them. So they could have their daily warm sausage roll and a coffee at a faction of the price, so they would not even be missing out!

The simple steps of being aware of the funds you have available and just thinking about what you are spending your money on before you spend it. Considering whether it is really needed or wanted and what you may be foregoing in the future by spending that money now, can make a real difference to your mind set and your spending habits.

Remember you will have worked hard for that money and forgone time with your family and friends to earn it.

If you went to a coffee shop for a take-out and someone said to you if you want this cup of coffee you need to do half an hour of work for it, would you still say yes to the coffee? Or would you rather go home and make your own cup of coffee at a lot lower cost.

If you had to work an hour for that cocktail or glass of wine would you still say yes?

If, when you consider what work you do for that money, you would still say yes that is fine, it is your money after all and enjoying what you work hard for is also important. Being savvy with your money is certainly not about saying no to everything, it is just about making sure you are happy with the choices you make.

Making sure you are thinking about whether you really need that coffee from the coffee shop around the corner, on your way into work, when your work supplies free tea and coffee. Or if you need that sandwich from a supermarket or deli when you could make yourself one at home and bring it to work. It is purely about thinking about it when you spend your money and confirming to yourself that yes that is a good thing to have spent that money on in your opinion. And knowing it is not leaving you short now or in the foreseeable future.

Thinking when you spend, whether that money could be used better for something else!

If you do spend some money on a whim and when you get

back home and think about it you regret it, don't beat yourself up over it, we all do it now and then. Let it go, but remember how you felt when you did regret it and think about that next time you are faced with a similar choice.

Whatever it is you have spent your money on, think whether that was a good or bad choice. You may find that it is an easy decision one way or the other. It may be an outright no I did not particularly enjoy it and I definitely would not want to spend that much money doing it again. That's an easy, don't do it again. Or you may have enjoyed it and felt more than comfortable spending the money you did on it, that's great and again an easy yes continue all the time you can afford to.

If, however, the money you have spent is disappointing and uncomfortable for you, but the thing you did was good and you want to be able to continue doing it, consider how you can do the same or similar for less. Set yourself a budget for it and work out a way to stick to it.

If, for example, you go out with friends every week so you love the social side and would not want to miss out, but you do not want to spend £X doing it, what could you change? Could you meet somewhere different, do a different activity, may be do the same thing just cheaper somewhere else.

If for example you go for a glass of wine each week with friends, and in addition you grab something to eat, then go for a few more drinks and then get a taxi back. Could you consider just doing the meal, so you save the money you would pay going on afterwards? Could you meet up after the meal so you save the meal costs? Could you drive so you save on the drink and the taxi? Could you get nibbles and a bottle of wine and invite your friends around?

Sometimes you just need to slightly change your mind set, you never know your friends might also be up for saving a bit of money and only go because they enjoy seeing you! So they may also be very open to changing it up.

There are many other options, including going out every other week, changing activity, go each week, but every other week you drive and just have a soft drink. It's just about thinking about alternative ways you can enjoy the same or similar and save money.

For those things you still want to continue spending your money on you just do not want to spend as much, look at all your options and pick the one that you think is the most ideal option for you.

Taking a firm control of your finances is not about stopping yourself doing anything other than paying your mortgage or rent and your bills and not having any fun at all. It is about learning to spend your money in a mindful and careful way and most importantly, spending it most effectively for you and your lifestyle. In addition it is about learning when you just have to say no sorry I can't do that this week or no I cannot buy this today.

Just make sure if you are spending money for the sake of spending it, make sure you are doing it intentionally. Do not find yourself spending it for the sake of spending it without even realising that is what you are doing.

If you do something regularly, daily, weekly, monthly, it is also worth working out what that costs you over a year and seeing if you are still happy to spend that amount annually on doing it. For example you may go out one night a week and spend £100, over a year are you really happy to have spent £5,200 on going out for that one night a week? If you are and you can afford to and there is really nothing else you would rather spend that money on that's good, carry on all the time you can afford to. If not, why not set yourself a budget for that activity, such as continuing to go out every week, but only spend a maximum of £50 a week, or decide to go out every other week and spend £100? Both these ways would save you £2,600 per year.

Again similar to when you try to spend as little as possible think what you could do with the unspent money, which would benefit you more. If holidays are already covered by your budget, it could be extra weekends away during the year. Money towards changing your car. Or with a sensible head on, paying off your mortgage earlier with regular over payments. You would probably save around half that again in interest over the term of your mortgage (depending on rates and term of mortgage). Obviously if you do decide to overpay your mortgage check your terms for what you can overpay by without being charged an early repayment fee.

If there is something you want to save for, without totally giving up your other activity. Decide what you would be willing to go without in order to save that money. Could you still go out but only spend £20 per week, if that's your target, work out how you can stick to your £20.

Think. Even if you do something that costs you £50 a month, that's £600 a year, that could be a nice little break for you and your family to make special memories together. And if the only thing you are giving up for that is a few pints of beer or a few glasses of wine a week it may be a no brainer.

As an added incentive, if you have a goal that you wish to save for, why not involve your loved ones, it will only help. If its saving for a family/friends holiday, planning a house move, whatever the dream is, doing it with others can make it easier as you can encourage each other to keep going.

Whatever your financial situation, being in control of your finances will be a great asset to you for the rest of your life. Gaining a greater understanding of your personal finances is only ever going to help you.

11 WHAT IF THE BALANCE IS NEGATIVE?

We touched on this above, what if the balance is negative? Do you give up at this stage, no of course not!

If, when you write down your income and your expenses you find your income is lower than the expenses you have listed, do not panic, remember being aware is the first step in taking control!

First consider is there any way you can sensibly increase your income? Are you due a raise? If so maybe now is the time to remind your boss, gently of course. Can you work more hours than you currently do?

Can you do a job from home in the evenings? If you take this option make sure you look into it thoroughly and that the job will in fact make you money. There are many work from home schemes that look like they should make you money, but actually do not. Make sure you fully understand what you are signing up for before you do and make sure you get an opinion from someone you trust.

Have you got a hidden talent you can unleash and make money from, sewing, drawing, making things? Maybe start your own little online business to supplement your income.

Even consider options you have for one off increases in income, such as a boot fair or using online sites for selling items. Most of us have things around the house we no longer use, but that have life left in them, start selling those items and turning them into cash, that will be useful now!

Take the other weekend, I cleared out my children's playroom and posted some items they no longer play with on a for sale site on a social media website. People came and collected the toys so I did not even need to leave the house and I made some money. My intention had only been to go through their playroom as it was becoming a mess, so the fact I managed to tidy up, make some money and someone else has the fun of having the toys to play with, was great.

It is so easy to do online and can even be free to advertise now!

This can give you a one off burst of cash in, but it is not something that can be done weekly or monthly to supplement your income.

If you need more money and there is nothing you can do to change the amount of money you have coming in, You will need to look into adjusting what you spend.

The first step would be to stop all unnecessary spending.

Now would be a great time to go through your expenses with a fine tooth comb. You can consider your essential costs and your non essentials looking for opportunities to save money. Be open to all avenues you see for reducing costs.

If you do not see any area you can save money, do not give up as it does not mean there are no options available to you, it just means there are none that you can think of at this point in time.

12 FIRST STEPS TO TIGHTING YOUR BELT.

As you have already written down everything that you spend that is essential and seen what it totals. Then added the other costs you have. Have a good look at these costs for areas where you can save money.

Obviously any luxuries should go first.

Some people may not even realise something they do is considered a luxury, especially if it is something they do not really think about. It is also different for different people, what is a luxury to one person may not be a luxury to another.

For example, I get a shop bought hair dye and buy my own nail varnish and I do it myself at home. For me going to a salon to get my hair coloured or my nails done is a real treat and something I do on special occasions if I can afford to. To someone else, such as a female flight attendant, it may be a necessity rather than a treat as it is essential, as part of their role as a flight attendant, to be immaculately presented.

Look at your list of out goings is there anything on it you consider a luxury, that you could reduce or cut out even if it is just for the time being, whilst you are trying to save money.

The other obvious expenses that people may believe should be the first to go, are sometimes the expenses that in a time like this, it feels the hardest to give up. For example if you smoke and or have the odd drink, if giving up is not an option, consider at least cutting down and just see what saving that would give you. It may surprise you what you could save and this in itself may spur you on to do even better.

There may be simple little changes that will not make that much difference to your life and the way you live it, but that can save you money.

If you currently buy your lunch at work, look into taking a packed lunch.

Do you have a TV subscription, if so, could you reduce the package you have to the parts you use most, or even cancel it completely?

If you have a gym membership, do you get your money's worth? If not consider cancelling and paying as you go. Maybe consider swapping to an exercise class or an exercise you can do yourself free of charge.

You may spend your money on a hobby and know what you are spending on it, but enjoy it, it keeps you fit and you wish to continue. If you have an expensive hobby, that you do regularly and over a year you spend a significant amount on it. You may want to continue, but like the idea of reducing the cost of it if you can.

Is there a way you can reduce your spending, but still enjoy the hobby the same? Could you buy your own equipment rather than hire it for example? Is there a membership that would give you cheaper access and as you do it enough it is worth purchasing? Can you get second hand equipment if buying new is too expensive? Can you get together with others that enjoy the same hobby and get group discounts when doing your hobby and share travel costs?

Look at your highest costs, even if these are your essential costs and ways you could reduce those. If you rent, is there a place that would work just as well for you, but would be cheaper to rent. If you have a mortgage consider swapping mortgage suppliers or product if possible, is there a cheaper mortgage you could get? Make sure you check any early repayment penalties of your existing product first though.

If you have finance or loans make sure you are not overpaying for it. If you have credit cards, store cards or payday loans, these are usually more expensive sources of finance, so look into the rates you are paying and if possible move your higher cost finance to lower cost finance. If you cannot do this, work on paying the higher cost finance off first.

For example if you have a high credit card bill, but have equity in your home, if you can remortgage without a penalty, consider the benefits of putting the debt on your lowest cost finance, your mortgage.

This is a way to make your debt more manageable, **but** if you do this then make sure you cut up your cards and do not get yourself straight back into the same position. You **must** also remember you will be paying your debt off over a longer period. So even though the finance cost will be lower in percentage terms you will be paying it for longer, so it may not be as cheap as you think over the full term of the debt. One way to help reduce this, if you take this option, is overpaying your mortgage when possible. Even if you are not able to do this for the foreseeable future bear it in mind for further in the future, when you may be in a position to.

Look into swapping utility suppliers if there is a cheaper option available, there are lots of online sites that help scour the utility companies for the best deals. If you do not have a computer yourself, ask someone you know that has one to help you. Or go to your local library where they have computers for the public to use and there are usually people that can help you if you are unsure about anything.

If you have a mobile phone contract consider other options, other contracts that are cheaper, maybe a reduced package. Do you use all the free calls, texts and data? Or even consider buying a phone and getting a sim only contract, this may cost more upfront, but will save money over the term of the contract and in the long run.

If you have a larger, thirstier car than you need consider trading it in and getting a reliable, efficient, cheaper to run car.

With your food shopping consider cutting out branded products where possible and reduce treats brought. Purchase food items that spread further, such as a meat joint that could be used for a roast and then a curry and then sandwiches for example. Look at cheap simple recipes to get ideas.

Consider cheaper supermarkets if you have access to them. Buy products whilst they are on offer and or in bulk as that can save money in the long term. Only do this if you know you need them and will use them.

Ordering your shopping online, to be delivered or picked up by click and collect, can avoid you seeing extra things and adding them to your trolley when you do not really need them.

If you are visiting a supermarket always take a list to the supermarket and try not to deviate from it. A list will help you focus and highlight when you are looking at items you do not need right now.

Making your own meals from scratch and your own bread, etc, can be cheaper than buying it from a store. Look into where you can incorporate this into your lifestyle.

Look at certain meals and how you could bring the price down.

Look at the discount shelves, some items can be taken home and frozen and used over time, especially things like bread, rolls, etc.

Be sure that you do not sacrifice healthier options for non-healthy options when you look at trying to save money on your food shopping.

Look at each cost you have and consider ways you could spend less.

Leave your credit/debit card at home. If you are going out take the cash you have to spend out with you and nothing else. If you are going somewhere you shouldn't spend money, don't take any with you. This makes its very difficult to spend more than you want and also makes you very conscious of what you are spending.

13 BE REALISTIC

You must be realistic.

It is no good kidding yourself that there are short cuts to saving money or paying off debt. Short cuts that are available relating to money are likely to be costly in the long run and therefore not beneficial for you, however good it seems and tempting it may be.

If you have a goal, recognise that the size of the goal, may affect the time it will take you to achieve it. Having an understanding of the timescale, by understanding your finances and knowing your options, can help you manage your expectations.

For example if you want to save for a suit or dress to wear to a wedding, you may be able to put half the money towards it this month and half next month, so your goal may be achieved in two months.

If your goal is larger, such as saving a deposit for a new home, it may be years in the making.

Knowing what your timescale is and what is involved, for the period of the timescale, is important.

This may all be about making sure you use the money you do have to the best of your ability, but let's also remember to be mindful that, as I have said before, there is more to life than money.

However, we would be kidding ourselves if we did not recognise that even though it is not as important as some things in our lives, as another saying says 'money makes the world go round,' so unfortunately, it is still a significant part of all our lives.

As I have already covered, but it does not hurt to mention again, when you think about the things that really matter to you, money will come a lot lower down the list than you may imagine. Having a loving supportive family, good health, true love, friends, honesty and happiness is not about money, but is actually what makes us rich. It is good to remind yourself of this regularly.

As the good old saying goes, 'money can't buy you love'!

14 BE MOTIVATED

It may be easier to motivate yourself to save for something, as the pleasure of what it is, is still to be had and should therefore motivate you to want to save for it.

Unfortunately it is not so easy when you are repaying money that you have already spent and had the pleasure of.

Remember:

It can be hard to repay debt so think of this before you take on debt.

If it is already too late as you have debt, remember how having the debt has made you feel, once you have got yourself straight, before you take on debt again.

You will get yourself straight if you are determined and motivated to.

Even if you are repaying debt, it is important that you feel motivated to succeed. The relief of seeing the route to being debt free will be a significant part of the motivation, but that alone may not be enough. There are ways to keep yourself motivated as you continue, during the process, especially if you begin to feel defeated.

If you are repaying debt, keep a running total so you can see the balance decreasing. Keep it somewhere you can access it easily and watch it coming down. Seeing the balance going down will be a large part of what will spur you on to continue.

If your debt is large it might be an idea to set certain goals and to give yourself a little treat as you get to each of them.

You may think why, this makes no sense, but bear with me as I do mean nothing extravagant, as that would be counterproductive. I am talking about something little, a well done, keep it going, you are doing great kind of a treat!

For example if you have a debt of £2,000 and you can pay it back at £100 a month, that's 20 months to repay in full. If you are having to forego say nights out to repay this, maybe at each £500 point, so every time you have paid £500 off, give yourself a reasonable budget to go out for an evening with friends.

If you are forgoing clothes to repay your debt, treat yourself to a new item of clothing when you hit your set targets, again within a reasonable budget.

In this example, it maybe that in month 6 you spend half your repayment (£50) on a treat. Be aware it would then take you 22 months to repay your debt, but keeping your motivation throughout the process is very important. So a treat may help the process run to completion and feel less painful. You may decide to have a month off paying your debt all together so you have £100 to treat yourself. So overall it would then take 24 months to repay your debt in full.

You need to work out what you realistically can do and what would motivate you best for achieving your goal of repaying the debt. Remember to keep it reasonable and not too expensive. It is a treat to keep you going and to say well done for getting to where you are.

This method gives you smaller goals to achieve, which will seem more attainable and it also gives you something to look forward to, as you will be able to treat yourself along the way. After forgoing something in order to repay debt it will feel good to have a little treat!

There may be a night out organised and you really want to go on it, but it would cost more than you would consider reasonable, in this case you could consider merging your treats together to allow you this one more special night. It's about motivation, so if this would motivate you that is fine, it is what works for you.

On the other hand you may feel so empowered by repaying your debt that when you get to the time you would treat yourself, you actually choose not to. That is fine. If you have the motivation without a treat that is great, its about keeping the motivation. Initially you can always consider the treat as postponed, rather than cancelled, so if you do get to a point where your motivation is dwindling, you are able to give yourself a little treat at that time.

If you do delay your treat and find your motivation fading, instead of going straight for the postponed treat try and push yourself a tiny bit further. Consider saying to yourself one more debt repayment then I will have the treat, just to give yourself that little extra goal to achieve, so you feel like you deserve your treat! You need it to be seen by yourself as a treat for success, rather than being fed up and giving in to spending money!

In choosing your motivational treat you will need to judge what you believe is reasonable and realistic and what target points you want to set for yourself. You will need to factor in what your treat means for your goal. In the above example the treats suggested would mean the completion of the goal would be delayed by 2-4 months.

If you cannot trust yourself to make the payments when they are due, set up a standing order direct from your bank account, so you are not having to process the transfer each month. This will avoid giving you the opportunity to not pay. If you have the option and feel it would help enlist the help of a family member or a friend, let them know what they could do to help you stay on track.

Finally, never give up! Stick to your plan and achieve it, even if you make a mistake during the plan, do not beat yourself up about it, chalk it down to experience and move on. Look forward not backwards. Rather than looking at what you have failed to achieve, look at what you have achieved.

Be proud of yourself.

This motivational technique can help with saving for something as well as paying off debt.

15 TURN UNWANTED STUFF INTO CASH!

Have you looked in your cupboards recently?

Gone through your children's toy boxes?

Ventured into your loft?

Gone through your garage or shed?

Have you got things sitting there unused and collecting dust, which someone else would pay good money for?

Clothes, bags, shoes, china, toys, material, bedding, pictures, frames, ornaments, soft furnishings, anything really.

As I touched on previously, one way to make money is to consider getting rid of anything you have that is in good condition, but you no longer need or want.

Use social media, as it is cheap and easy, to help you sell your unwanted items.

As the saying goes one person's rubbish (unwanted items) is another person's treasure!

If you have a lot of unwanted items consider doing a boot fair. If you are not sure see if a friend wants to do one too. When I do a boot fair I do it with a very good friend of mine and it can actually be quite good fun.

Online sites are better for fewer higher priced items and boot fairs for a larger number of cheaper items. That is not to say you could not sell something cheaper online, or something more expensive at a boot fair. It is just about making a judgement of what would be better for you and the items you have to sell.

As well as the playroom toys I mentioned earlier, in the summer, we had a plastic play house and sand pit our kids had, had for years. That they had not used for the last couple of years. I gave them a quick clean and put a post on a social media for sale site, within minutes I had a lot of messages of people interested. Within a couple of days they had been picked up and we got the asking price.

Unfortunately on this occasion it was not spare cash to be frivolous with as in the meantime my children had managed to rip the mat of their trampoline. So the funds we got for the playhouse and sandpit were put away towards a new trampoline. It was good to have well over half our budget for the trampoline from selling stuff no longer used by us, that has lots of life still left in it for others to enjoy. These odd costs always seem to come out of the blue, especially if you have children, so it is good to have a way of covering them that does not necessarily effect the way you live.

You actually get two benefits from getting rid of unused things. There is not a lot that is more satisfying than doing a life laundry on your home and garden. Getting rid of the things you no longer need or use. Getting space back in your home and of course getting some extra cash in your pocket.

Once you have gone through your belongings and cleared out everything you are prepared to sell you can be very proud of yourself. If you are left with bits that you have not been able to sell, consider giving them away online FREE, or giving them to charity, whichever is your preference. If the value is too high for you to be able to consider that, put it by and try to sell it again another week. I put some of my children's toys on and one lot did not sell, I put it on again and it did not sell, I put it on a month later and it went straight away. It was not to do with the price as that was the same each time, but obviously just depends if the right person is looking.

16 REMEMBER THE THINGS IN LIFE THAT ARE FREE.

There are a lot of things that are free in this world, things that can give us some of the best days out and memories. We need to embrace these things now, in the present.

If you feel like you want to do something, but have limited or no funds, why not get creative with your time.

Exercise for free.

If you are looking to exercise, why not go for a walk, jog or run. Or even make your own exercise routine at home or in your garden. The traditional press up, sit up, star jump, plank, exercises are still used in most classes today. Do you need to pay someone to tell you to do ten or can you just tell yourself this is what you are going to do.

You can also get ideas of different types of exercises online, or if you have been to a class before think about what you did there. Pick the exercises you did not like (burpees in my case) as well as the ones you may have liked. So you make sure you do challenge yourself.

You could borrow an exercise DVD or look on YouTube (or similar) if you need inspiration or something to follow.

Enlist a family member or a friend who likes to keep fit so you have company and added motivation.

You can switch what you do each time to keep you interested.

Meeting up with friends.

If you want to catch up with friends, arrange to go for a walk, or go round to a friends for a cuppa or invite your friend round. Walking or sitting and chatting, it doesn't matter where you are if you enjoy each other's company you will have a lovely time. It doesn't always have to be over a meal or drink out.

In the Spring and Summer what could be nicer than sitting outside in your garden catching up with friends.

I sometimes meet up with my best friend on the beach with our dogs, we take a flask and pack of biscuits from home and can sit there for hours. We have sat on the beach, whilst our dogs run around having the time of their lives, in both glorious sunshine and chilly rain and have had a lovely time. Or met with our kids at a park with a picnic.

These days you can get lots of messages/invites about days or nights out that have been arranged, don't feel obliged to do everything. Think about getting in early if you want to suggest a cheap or FREE option. Don't feel you can't let your friends know you cannot afford to do something, they may be feeling the same.

Getting outside.

If you want to get out and about, if you are lucky enough to live near a beach, a park or a wood, getting in the fresh air, whatever the weather, can be very good for the soul and really lift your spirits.

Gardening, kids like to help so get them involved with a little spade/trowel.

Swimming in the sea in the Summer months is so exhilarating.

A fresh crisp winter walk makes you feel good to be alive.

Whether you choose to go for a stroll or you just wish to sit or lay and relax and maybe read a book. It's a lovely way to spend a few hours.

Nature has a fantastic way of helping us feel grounded and again is free for us to enjoy!

If it's evenings you are thinking about, in the summer why not make a picnic and head to a park or the beach and watch the sun set. Or even a picnic or meal in your garden will do the trick if you have no easy access to public spaces.

Evenings or afternoon in.

Movie night in, borrow a DVD or if you have a film option in your current TV package that costs you no extra, snuggle down for a chilled evening in.

Have a bubble bath and read a good book.

Simple things you can spend an afternoon doing, such as playing a board game, doing a puzzle or playing cards. If you don't own any of these, make up your own game.

The postit game where you put a character or person on a postit on each others head and then have to guess who you are, is fun and loved by all ages. Each time you ask a question and it is correct you get to ask another question. If you get it wrong the next person gets to start asking questions about who they are.

My children like doing games at the dinner table, such as naming countries starting with each letter of the alphabet. Starting with A and going round each person at the table again and again until you get to Z. Be warned there are no countries beginning with X.

This game we have also done with names, animals, foods, etc.

Another easy game is the name game where you have to say a name with the last letter of the name the person before you said.

Game nights as well as afternoons can be great fun!

Local amenities

What does your local area offer you?

Libraries are free and they have DVD's as well as books to loan out. Why not walk to your local library stay and sit peacefully in the reading corner deciding what books you want to take out, or just pick up your chosen books and leave. A visit to the library is equally nice for adults and children and if we do not use them one day they may no longer be there for us, so support your local library.

Play parks, woods, local walks. Investigate what your area has to offer and enjoy what they do! Lots of areas have groups that go for walks together, so if you are looking for good walks and some company why not look into whether your area does something like this.

Look out for local events that are free, they often put flyers up or a booklet through the door to advise of these types of events. Social media also advertise events in your local area.

Check out local boot fairs, it can be fun to walk around even if you do not want to buy anything. If you do end up buying something it will no doubt be a bargain (so why not, this once!).

What about your local Church, you may not follow any religion, but churches are often very welcoming and if you are looking to become part of your community they are a good place to go.

Childcare & Babysitting

Childcare can be very expensive. It can be the reason some parents cannot go back to work even if they want to. Grandparents can often be worth their weight in gold and step in to help out. My mum has helped us out since my eldest was 8 weeks old and I will always be eternally grateful as we could not have done it without her.

When I was younger, as my younger siblings are 10 years younger than me, I helped my mum out with child care for short periods of time when she needed to leave home to get to her evening job, but my dad was not back from work. So it doesn't necessarily have to be a grandparent, it can be any responsible relative.

If you are not in the fortunate position to have a relative that can help out, talk to other parents you know in similar situations and consider trading childcare with each other. This can work very well especially if you have school age children and need to work during the school holidays.

If you have a night out planned, babysitting can double the cost of your night out meaning it is no longer viable to go, so again if you have family and friends that can help that's great. My parents, siblings and friends help us out with babysitting, I do the same for them, it is nice to know you can help.

I have also had to call on some of my lovely mummy friends when a school pick up or drop off has become a problem at the last minute. I cannot speak highly enough about having a great support group, where it works both ways, it is invaluable.

Entertaining young children.

Remember that more than anything else, they love just spending time with you so you do not have to be extravagant.

Often when your kids tell you about their favourite days it will be days they spent with you and when you think back to lovely days you have had, I imagine you mostly think of the simple pleasures. Reading a book with your child, snuggling down to watch a movie, playing in the garden, going to the park or the beach, going on a bike ride. You remember the time together not the things you have bought for them and so do they.

Whether it is building dens at home, reading together, playing a game, doing a puzzle, colouring or painting. Going for a walk and finding sticks, or kicking leaves, or jumping in puddles. Going to the beach and throwing stones in the sea and paddling. Walking around the local woods or park, or just going out and spotting things. Kids enjoy company.

Younger kids love play parks if you have one close by, even half an hour at a play park can feel like the best day ever to a child.

Playing a simple game of ball in the garden.

If your children have a bike or scooter, taking them around the block on them, is great fun.

Social Media may have its negatives, but it also has its positives, people not only sell stuff they also give stuff away that still has life in it. It may not be brand new in condition, but you may be able to grab some games or toys for your children for nothing.

The other weekend we gave away, a climbing frame, a small girl's bike and seesaw for nothing. They were not in brilliant condition, but they did still have loads of life left in them. Granted the lady who wanted it and was first to say, had to collect it, so in these cases you may need access to transport, but then she had three quite costly items that would provide many months/years of play for her children!

These free goods may not come up every day, but it is certainly worth keeping an eye out as I often see free items on for sale sites online.

Passing on or borrowing

Whether it is clothes, toys or books it is good to pass on the things your children have grown out of. If you know someone with older kids they will probably be happy to pass on their kids clothes and things, that are still in good condition, to your children once they have grown out of them.

My sister has two older girls and has always passed on their clothes to my daughter. I then pass them on to my god daughter and she passes them on to her cousins.

It's not only for kids though. My sister who shops for clothes and bags more often than I do and quite often has a clear out of her wardrobe, passes on some of her clothes to me. It's great as even though they have been preloved they are new to me and are a welcome addition to my wardrobe.

Never feel that you always need to get new, used can be just as good. Some of the items my sister has given me have become my favourite go to items.

If you have a group of friends from a toddler group, why not get them round for a coffee morning and clothe swap?

Borrowing an item instead of buying is another option you should explore. If you only need the item once why not see if someone already has one that you could borrow. A suit, you may need for one event and they are expensive to buy so ask around your friends and family, see if they have one you can borrow for the occasion. It is the same with dresses, shoes, bags, fascinators, etc. It even extends to tools or tents for camping trips. Often people that have spent money on these items are only too happy for them to be used.

I borrowed a ball gown once from a very lovely friend of mine, which was gorgeous. I got so many compliments during the evening and felt amazing. It was no doubt a dress that was worth well over £100 and I got to wear it and feel wonderful. I have to be honest, I did get the dress dry cleaned (£20) and I wanted to give my friend a token of my appreciation, so I got her a bottle of Prosecco (£7). So granted I spent a little, but I wore a dress that far exceeded anything I would have purchased and made me feel great. In addition as I do not get the opportunity to go to places where I could wear a ball gown very often, if I had purchased a dress it would be in my wardrobe having only been worn once, so this worked perfectly for me!

I have been the other side, where I bought a lovely dress once for £80, I wore it once, loved it, but I did not get the opportunity to wear it again. I tried to sell it online it did not sell, I tried to sell it at a boot fair, at the end of the boot fair when I was having to load my unsold stuff back into the car, which is the horrible part, someone offered me £1 for it and as I thought its only going to hang in my wardrobe I took the £1. In hindsight maybe I should have tried to sell online again, or given it to charity. Basically when I borrowed a dress worth well over £100 it cost me £27 to wear it and feel wonderful for that night out, when I purchased and wore a dress that cost £80 it cost me £79 to wear the dress and feel lovely that night! Obviously you have to have a friend that has similar taste in clothes, is the same or very similar in size and who is kind enough to let you borrow it!

Bags for life

I cannot be the only one that has hundreds of bags for life!!! I keep them in my car boot as well as in a cupboard at home and I still go into the shop without them so I have to purchase more on a regular occurrence. *Remember* your bag for life when you go shopping !!! They may not be free initially, but they are free to reuse!

Finally

Something that is totally free, it seems too simple to even write, but I am going to as sometimes I think we need reminding that daylight is free! The amount of times I will go into my children's rooms and they have their curtains drawn and their lights or lamps on, even though it is daylight outside. Let's get those lights turned off when they are not needed and make the most of the free and beautiful daylight. Save some money on electric too!

17 SWAP COSTLY OPTIONS FOR CHEAPER OPTIONS.

As I mentioned earlier in the book it's not necessarily about missing out on things, sometimes there are good alternatives that are a lot cheaper.

If you rent a house consider other rental properties in your area that may be cheaper.

If you have a mortgage, swap providers, but check costs and fee's thoroughly first. Or consider moving to a cheaper house/area.

Swap insurers & utility companies annually to keep your premium/costs down.

Does your bank offer you a reward account, if so look into it and talk to them about whether it would benefit you. I have one and I get back monthly at least 3 times the amount it costs to have it just by paying my bills , which I have to pay anyway!

If you have to have a credit card swap for a cheaper card if possible.

As mentioned previously, swap for a lower cost car. Even once you have purchased a car you have to pay the ongoing costs such as petrol/electric, RFL, insurance, services, MOT's, so make sure the car you pick has a good track record and is in your budget in terms of running costs as well as the initial purchase.

If you are considering missing out on University due to the cost. Consider the longer term benefits of getting the career you hope for, which might be worth the student loan repayments in the grand scheme of things. Remember if you haven't repaid the loans in 30 years the current rules mean you stop repaying after that time. It is really like an extra tax, but if you get a better career because of going to University it could still make sense. You may be able to reduce your costs of University if for example your preferences are a University miles away from home, consider a more local one, that you could maybe travel to daily to reduce your living costs.

Never give up on your dream to become what you want to become, so if University is not an option for you, consider the Open University, where you can study at home.

Swap a coffee shop coffee for a coffee at home.

Swap a few drinks out for a catch up with friends and a few drinks in.

Swap a trip to your local café for making cakes at home, cheaper and much more fun.

Swap a take away or trip to a restaurant for pizza making at home or even shop bought pizza.

Swap a trip to the cinema for film nights at home with popcorn.

Swap romantic meals out for romantic meals in, candles and all.

Swap a day trip to the beach, if you are not local to the beach, for a paddling pool, sprinkler and ice cream in the garden.

Swap an exercise class for a work out on the trampoline in your garden if you have one and get all the family involved.

Swap a gym membership for a regular jog.

Swap a clothes shopping trip for a friends, bring and swap party, at home, this can be for both kids and adult clothes.

Swap expensive clothes & shoe shops for cheaper shops, even supermarkets are pretty good these days, they often have at least a few nice items at even greater prices. Or swap for a charity shop, not only can you find some real bargains the money you do spend goes to a good cause.

When you do buy clothes, learn to buy items that mix and match well, so you can make several outfits out of them. Also items that are flexible, that you can dress down and dress up.

Swap a salon for a mobile hairdresser.

Swap supermarket if you have a lower price supermarket local to you.

Swap new books for going to library or swapping books with family and friends.

Swap games with other families you know, to mix up games afternoon.

Swap an expensive day trip to the zoo for a day trip to a not so costly farm.

If you earn points at a supermarket and can swap points for day trips, look into what day trips you could do. This works well for travel as well.

Swap a new outfit, for borrowing an outfit from a family or a friend.

Swap a spa day for a face mask, relaxing music and a chill at home.

Swap light bulbs for lower energy ones.

Swap shop bought gifts for homemade gifts.

Repair holes in clothes rather than throwing them away.

Swap an exercise class for an exercise DVD. You will find in a lot of cases you only have to do the DVD a handful of times to have more than made your money back and most of us can stick it out that long.

Swap a slimming club, for your own slimming club with friends, you can do your own weigh in's weekly and research online healthy recipes that you share with each other.

Share rides to work. Car-pooling has been around for a ages, but I expect there are still loads of us that come practically right past a colleagues door without sharing transport. Even better if you can walk or cycle to work, stop driving all together.

Swap brand new for used, shop around. With Ebay, social media, local papers, charity shops, boot fairs, etc, it is so much easier to grab a bargain these days, especially as we are a throwaway society. It may seem difficult at first, if you are used to brand new, but give it a go and I am sure you will be a convert. Whether its toys, school uniform, clothes, furniture, etc there are many good second hand options these days.

Swap trades, if you can do something someone else cannot, but they have a skill you need, consider swapping your trades. This can even be for something like babysitting.

Grow your own vegetables. A pack of seeds will last you a good while, make sure you plant something you eat regularly. I grew rocket, which I love and at less than £3 for the seeds or £1 a packet of rocket, I was certainly in pocket as I had a great crop for a good period of time. Also spinach has been very successful for me. Both were simple to plant and look after. I still have spinach growing now it seems to survive the hardest of conditions, as we have had a very warm summer and snow this winter.

Do not shy away from trying to use your leftovers to make them into a delicious meal. With the internet these days it's easy to get a great range of recipes.

My children have had second hand bikes, they have all been in great condition clean and scratch free, as we are selective. They have been in full working order and we have even been able to sell them on at the end or pass them down. It would make no difference to the fun they have on them, if they were brand new, but it would make a serious difference to the cost.

Take picnics on days out rather than going to a café or fast food restaurant.

It is also a good idea to look out for deals in newspapers, online, on packaging to save money on days out.

Use coupons, if you buy a product regularly and you get a coupon, keep it and use it next time.

Buy refills, which are often cheaper than buying the product again as the packaging is cheaper. Hand soap is a good item to buy refills for.

Shop in the sales, if after Christmas you have birthdays coming up, plan ahead, buy presents in the sale to get more for your money. If you have money to put by in January towards the following Christmas, there is no reason why you cannot spend it in the sales and put the presents away till Christmas.

As you can see planning ahead is not only about knowing what money you have to spend, it can also help you get the same products for less.

Shop in sales – January sales – I have already mentioned planning ahead for birthday and Christmas presents, but you can take this further and plan ahead for holiday clothes, work clothes etc.

In addition you should try and avoid buying high priced clothing that you will only wear once! If you need that special outfit for a wedding and you really don't want to or cannot borrow, even if the wedding is not until the summer plan ahead and buy one in the sales in January.

Not only will this make you super organised, it will also save you money!! Win, win.

Finally, if you have something that has broken, do not always assume it needs replacing, consider fixing it. I have to be honest I am very guilty of thinking 'oh no I need to buy a new one' the minute something gets broken, luckily my husband is handy when it comes to things like this, he looks into what part is broken and if it can be fixed. Nine times out of ten it can be. My hair straighteners are over 10 years old and on their third lead, but still going strong, *touch wood*! If you are not handy when it comes to fixing things and you don't have a relative or friend that could help you, there are many online video's that can help you learn how to fix a whole range of things. Obviously only do this if it is something within your capabilities, never put yourself at any risk.

18 TAKE NOTE OF REVIEWS & ADVANTAGE OF INCENTIVES

Sometimes though we do have to accept that it is worth paying more for things and that shopping cheaper is a false economy.

For example I bought my daughter a pair of boots for school the style was good, they turned up looking nice, they were from a high-street store I had heard of, but not used before. Within days the upper of the boots was badly scratched and within a month the sole had come away at the toes on both boots.

I then invested in a more expensive pair from a different high-street store that I have used before and trust their quality and they have lasted the whole rest of the winter and still look good.

Two pairs of the cheap boots would have cost the same as one pair of the better quality boots, therefore if I had gone for the better quality, more expensive one from the start I would have only had to buy one pair of boots. So in reality they were cheaper because the life of the item was longer and it was needed to be longer.

It may not have mattered had the poor quality boots been party or occasional shoes they may have lasted the period they were required for.

This is not to say cheaper is worse as it is not, but if you are shopping different brands for something that you hope will last a certain amount of time and that will get a lot of wear and tear it makes sense to know the item you are buying is fit for purpose. With so many review sites being available to us now it makes sense to look at reviews before making a final decision.

Make sure you read reviews if you are going for a brand you have not tried before, talk to other people, that may have purchased similar items, to find out about their experiences. The picture may look perfect, but if the reviews are negative read them and make your decision.

Also ask your friends and family – social media gives you a platform to get opinions almost instantly, if you are thinking of buying something or going away somewhere ask for opinions.

If you are going to make a purchase from a new site and you have not heard anything about them, again ask people before you commit.

When you shop both in store and online you will often find you are offered incentives to get you to join mailing lists or set up an account, if you can be strict with yourself, taking advantage of incentives can save you money.

I recently set up an account which gave me the option to pay later, I actually wanted to buy the item there and then, but the offer came with £10 off so I signed up. At the first opportunity I got I paid it off in full. I even set a reminder in my calendar to make sure I did not forget to pay it in full.

The account also then offered me a further £10 discount as a welcome when I used the account the next time after signing up, again I took advantage of the discount, but I paid the full balance off at the first opportunity. If I had not signed up I would have spent £20 more on my purchases. I did not let it encourage me to spend more or get things I did not really want or need, but I used the discount to reduce my costs.

Offers of money off if you sign up now can save you money if and only if you can use it sensibly.

You may be surprised to see I am going to talk pensions in this section of the book, but I think its as good a place as any to discuss this. All workplaces have to offer a Workplace pension scheme to their employee's (you must meet the criteria). If you are employed and you have been automatically enrolled to a pension scheme and you have decided to opt out. Have you thought it through? If you put 5% in your company has to put 3% in and you get tax relief on your contribution. For example if you earn £1,000 per month, you would need to put in £50 per month in the pension. This, however, is split 80% from you and 20% from tax relief, so basically you put in £40 the tax man puts in £10 and your company puts in £30. So by spending £40, you get £80 in your pension. That is an incentive to sign up! If you do not sign up you lose the 3% employer contribution as an employer cannot give you it as additional salary. So its pension or nothing.

19 BEING PREPARED FOR COSTLY TIMES OF YEARS.

Nothing will serve you better than planning ahead for costly times of year.

Save during the year where you can, it is not like birthdays or Christmas are a surprise.

If it is in your budget and you have money put by for it, by the time it comes around, it makes the costly months much easier to handle.

If you spend £500 on presents at Christmas, put £42 away each month, if you spend £2000, put £167 away each month.

If you have ten birthdays you have to buy for during the year, work out how much you spend on birthdays in total and make sure you put a monthly amount away. In this case you need to be careful that the birthdays do not come in advance of you having the money put by. For example if you start saving in January, but four out of the ten birthdays are in January, you will not have the money you need by that time, so you need to factor this in to your savings.

If you get a bonus at work, put some or all of it towards your costly times of year.

If you do a boot fair or sell stuff online and the money you get is not already allocated put it by for your costly time of year.

At costly times of year, especially Christmas, it is important to manage people's expectations when it comes to gifts they can expect. This can be done simply by suggesting a limit to spend on each other. This is what my sister and I do as we both have a husband and children so for Christmas we put a limit on what we spend on each other's family members including each other.

With your children you could give them some pages out of a catalogue and tell them to list their favourite top five items and that Santa will buy them one off their list. Then you can always ask family to buy some of the other items when they ask for ideas.

Shops at Christmas compete for your custom, so shop around to make sure you are getting the best deal.

If you have purchased presents earlier in the year to spread the cost and may be to take advantage of sales, make sure you put them somewhere you remember you purchased them. Write a list of who you need to buy for and as you buy for each of them note down what you have bought for them. Then you can refer back to it when you want to know who else you need to buy for and what you have already purchased. This should stop you double buying, or forgetting anyone.

I found some girl's ballerina notebooks I had purchased in advance for my daughters friends, then forgot about and purchased gifts as their birthdays came round! So I make sure I keep a list I update as required.

Learn to say no. People understand when you are having an expensive time of year so if you are invited out and you really cannot afford to go, don't feel you have to go and put strain on yourself to find the money. Explain that it's an expensive time of year and you can't make it as you have other commitments you are already tied to.

If you plan to go on the most nights out you can, but your budget will only stretch so far, go on the cheaper ones and resist the more expensive evenings. A girly catch up round a friends, may involve taking some food and drink and getting a taxi home. An evening out may involve a meal, drinks, entertainment and taxi, as well as a new outfit. Work out what works for you and for your budget and stick to it!

I have four family birthdays in one month, so not only is it a very busy month for me, it is also very expensive even when I plan ahead. So usually when I am invited out during that month, I have to say no, but my friends totally understand and yours will too.

Other costs that may not be monthly, but again should not be a surprise include:

> TV licences
> Car MOT
> Car service
> Holidays
> Trips away
> Annual vet bills
> Valentines
> Mother's day
> Father's day
> Anniversaries

If you know it's the month your car MOT is due, you are going on holiday, or whatever the cost may be, make sure you are as prepared as you can be financially, save a little each month and restrict your spending in that month.

If you expect your car MOT to be £100, put away £8.50 a month towards it. If your holiday is going to be £1000 including spending, put by £83.33 per month.

Do not be tempted to use the money you have put by on a whim. That money is to help you meet future costs you know you have. If you find yourself in a position where you do need to dip into it as you have no other alternative, make sure you set yourself a plan that replenishes the borrowed funds in a timely manner so your finances do not start to snowball.

20 IF YOU NEED ADDITIONAL FINANCE.

Hopefully this will not be the case, but if you have followed all the tips already mentioned. Budgeting, planning, swapping more expensive for less expensive options, enjoying life's things that are free. Sorting stuff you no longer need and selling it. Limiting your out goings and increasing your income as much as you are able to. However, you still find yourself in a position that you do need help financially, where should you go?

First consider, are you entitled to an extra help financially, speak to someone at the benefits office or have a look online. Whether you are employed or not there may be some additional financial help available.

If this is not an option.

Refer back to chapter 11, 'What if the balance is negative?'. Remember speaking to someone can really help and if you do not have close family and friends that you can seek advice from, there are organisations that can provide advice and support, reach out to them.

If you need extra funds, work out how long you need the money for and how much it is.

If it is short term or a relatively small amount consider if you have any options for an interest free loan. In terms of a loan from family or friends, or if you have access to an interest free credit card?

If so an interest free option has to be the favourite option. If you go for the interest free credit card, make sure you are going to be able to pay it off within the interest free terms and do not get lulled into a false sense of security and believing you have more funds available than you do.

If you do not have an interest free option, consider the cheapest option you have available?

Consider all the options you have and go for the cheapest and most suitable. Make sure it is the easiest and/or quickest to pay off.

If it is a longer term requirement you have, again you need to look at your options and follow the same process as for short term finance.

Make sure before you sign up to any loans, be it an informal loan from your family or a bank loan, that you have a set plan in place for repaying it.

21. IF YOU HAVE SPARE MONEY

If once you have paid everything you need to, both essential and non essential costs, you have spare funds, look into what to do with those funds to make them work for you.

Make sure you look at spare funds once you have paid off any debt in full, *with the exception of your mortgage,* before you consider saving and investing. You will probably find the debt costs you more than any income you will get saving and on investments. Therefore it is a sound decision not to save and invest all the time you are paying off a high interest loan or credit card, as the money would be better spent paying off the debt!

For example if you have a loan where you pay 8% per annum and the opportunity to invest with a 6% per annum return, it makes sense to pay more off the debt which you are being charged 8% on than to invest in something that will give you 6% return.

If you are debt free, (other than mortgage) and still have spare funds now is the time to consider saving and investing.

The safest place to put your money is in a savings accounts. They all have different rates, different tie in's and different tax implications. So look into what suits you, the level of funds you have and the length of time you can leave the funds tied up.

With ISA's you can have a cash ISA and a stocks & shares ISA, there are many different suppliers so look into both types and the most suitable suppliers for you, before deciding which is best.

Have you already got a pension you included in your essential or non essential costs? If so, could you consider increasing your contributions? If not, with these spare funds could it be time to start one?

If you already have a pension and savings and the only debt you have is your mortgage. One option would be to overpay on your mortgage, however if you have a competitive rate you may decide paying it off early is not something you wish to do. You may also believe there are investments that could produce a return greater than the interest rate you pay on your mortgage. So an investment opportunity may suit you.

Are you interested in investing in shares, domestic or commercial property, business opportunities, bonds, gilts? Whatever you may wish to invest in make sure you know the risks and are comfortable with them before you invest your money. Always consider the worse case option and make sure that based on the reward that you could gain, the worst case scenario, although maybe not palatable, is worth the risk.

Hedge your bets, you know the saying don't put all your eggs in one basket. It is sound advice.

If you are unsure what to do with the money you have and unsure in your own ability and knowledge to make a decision when it comes to investing, consider speaking to a financial advisor to see how they could help you decide where best to invest your money.

If you have spare cash it is not all about investing. Consider spending the money on things you have wanted to do. You may have your holidays covered but are there other places you have wanted to visit. Its important to live life and make memories as that is what we are left with in the end!

CONCLUSION

Now you are at the end of this book, consider what your reason for reading this book was and hopefully it will allow you to achieve whatever it was you were hoping for.

Hopefully this book will have given you ideas of how to live the best life you can whatever your income.

Know that doing the same thing and expecting a different outcome is futile, so you will need to change what you do if you are looking for a different outcome.

Acknowledge what you want to achieve.

Understand the time it will take to achieve your goal.

Break down your goal into smaller steps if needs be.

Learn from this book that everyone has options open to them, even if they seem harder to identify initially.

Use this book for reference as you go forward to meet your financial goals.

Know the power is in your own hands.

Do what the majority of us crave to do, live well, spend less.

ABOUT

THE AUTHOR

Alana Wilson is a 45 year old Chartered Accountant who has worked in both practice and industry. She wanted to become an Accountant from the age of eleven and completed her degree at the University of Hertfordshire in Accounting and Management Information Systems before working in practice whilst studying with the ICAEW. She lives in the South East of England with her Husband, three awesome children and their lively cockapoo. This is the first book she has written as she was keen to use her experience and knowledge to help others.

Printed in Poland
by Amazon Fulfillment
Poland Sp. z o.o., Wrocław

49386290R00058